Community, Culture, and Me

Written by Gavin Worthy

Rules and Laws

KidHaven PUBLISHING

Published in 2027 by
KidHaven Publishing, an Imprint of Greenhaven Publishing, LLC
2544 Clinton St., Buffalo, NY 14224

Written by: Gavin Worthy
Edited by: Doug Barone
Designed by: Ker Ker Lee

Cataloging-in-Publication Data

Names: Worthy, Gavin.
Title: Rules and laws / Gavin Worthy.
Description: Buffalo, NY : KidHaven Publishing, 2027. | Series: Community, culture, and me | Includes glossary and index.
Identifiers: ISBN 9781534569980 (pbk.) | ISBN 9781534569997 (library bound) | ISBN 9781534570009 (ebook)
Subjects: LCSH: Communities--Juvenile literature. | Communities--Law and legislation--Juvenile literature.
Classification: LCC HM756.W678 2027 | DDC 307--dc23

Printed in China

CPSIA compliance information: Batch #QS27KH: For further information contact Greenhaven Publishing LLC at 1-844-317-7404

Please visit our website, www.greenhavenpublishing.com.
For a free color catalog of all our high-quality books, call toll free 1-844-317-7404 or fax 1-844-317-7405.

Find us on

Photo Credits – Images courtesy of Shutterstock.com, unless otherwise stated.

Cover & Recurring – Rawpixel.com, PeopleImages.com, Dedraw Studio, TVhappyLine, kinder my, christinarosepix, Evgeny Atamanenko. 2–3 – Media_Photos. 4–5 – Dennis MacDonald, Dorde Krstic. 6–7 – yMelnikov Dmitriy, Alexandros Michailidis. 8–9 – wavebreakmedi, PeopleImages. 10–11 – John Gomez, antoniodiaz. 12–13 – Gorodenkoff, AnnaStills. 14–15 – PeopleImages, Dragon Images. 16–17 – ARMMY PICCA, Tirachard Kumtanom. 18–19 – SeventyFour, Tony Marturano. 20–21 – Ground Picture, Rawpixel.com. 22–23 – PeopleImages.

Contents

Words that look like **this** can be found in the glossary on page 24.

Rules to Follow

Rules tells us what we are allowed or not allowed to do. People follow rules every day. You might have a list of rules about how to act in the classroom.

Can you think of some rules you have to follow?

You probably have rules at home too. You might have rules about screen time. If you break the rules, it might mean you will be disciplined.

Have you ever been disciplined for breaking a rule?

What Is a Law?

A law is a rule that every person in a certain place must follow. Some laws are meant to keep society peaceful. There are seirous punishments for breaking these laws.

Laws are made by the **government** of a city, state, or country. Usually, laws are written down and agreed on by members of the government. Sometimes, countries come together to make bigger rules that help the whole world.

Why Do We Need Rules and Laws?

Rules help keep us safe. Think of a "no running" rule in a school—this rule stops people from getting hurt by falling over or running into people. Laws are meant to keep people safe too.

Rules also make sure everyone is treated fairly. You might have rules that say you must share things with others. This helps everyone get along peacefully. Laws can also help make things fair.

There are even laws that protect people's right to speak freely.

Police

Police officers have many jobs. They make sure everybody follows the rules. They stop people who are breaking the law. People who break the law are called criminals.

Police officers should help people. It is important that they treat everyone fairly. Police officers around the world also follow rules to make sure they act properly.

Courts

If the police say someone has broken the law, that person may go to court. In court, people hear what happened and decide whether that person has broken the law.

Sometimes there is a jury in court. This is a group of randomly chosen people who decide if a law was broken. A judge generally decides what the punishment will be.

Punishment

There are different punishments for breaking laws. Some people must pay money, which is called a fine. Other people must do unpaid work, such as cleaning. This is called **community** service.

Community service makes criminals give back to the communities they harmed.

Some people go to prison. Criminals must stay in prison for a certain amount of time. The amount of time is often based on the kind of law they broke. Some workers in prisons help criminals learn to make better choices.

Fair for All

Some laws are meant to make sure everyone in a community is treated fairly and equally.

This statue is used as a **symbol** for the law. The scales show how the law should be balanced and equal.

Throughout history, women have not been treated equally to men. Many countries now have laws to make sure women are treated fairly, such as by being paid as the same as men for doing the same job.

Unfair for Some?

Sometimes, rules need to change. Rules and laws that were made a long time ago might actually be very unfair. New laws might also be needed.

In some countries, marriage was only allowed between a man and a woman. However, lots of countries changed their laws so that people could marry whomever they wanted. Many people support these new laws.

It is unfair to have one rule for some people and another rule for others.

Making Change

Laws can be changed by the government. People can show their government that they want a law to change in many ways. They can sign a petition or go to a protest.

During protests, people might wave signs and chant in a public place.

People can help change rules and laws by voting. There are many different ways of voting. People can vote for government leaders.

Sometimes, people write their votes on paper and put them in a box.

Your Rules

It's time to use what you have learned in this book to think about the rules in your life. What do you think are the most important rules to follow?

Are there any rules that you think are missing?

Think of all the rules you have to follow. Is there a rule that you would change? Why would you change that rule, and how would you go about changing it?

If you were in charge of a country, what laws would you make?

Glossary

community	a group of people who are connected by something
government	the group of people with the power to run a country and decide its laws
petition	something that asks for a change, which lots of people write their names on to show they also want this change
public	open to people in the community
punishments	things that are done to people who have done something wrong to teach them not to do it again
randomly	not having a pattern or a reason
society	a collection of people living together at a certain time
symbol	a thing that is used to stand for something else

Index